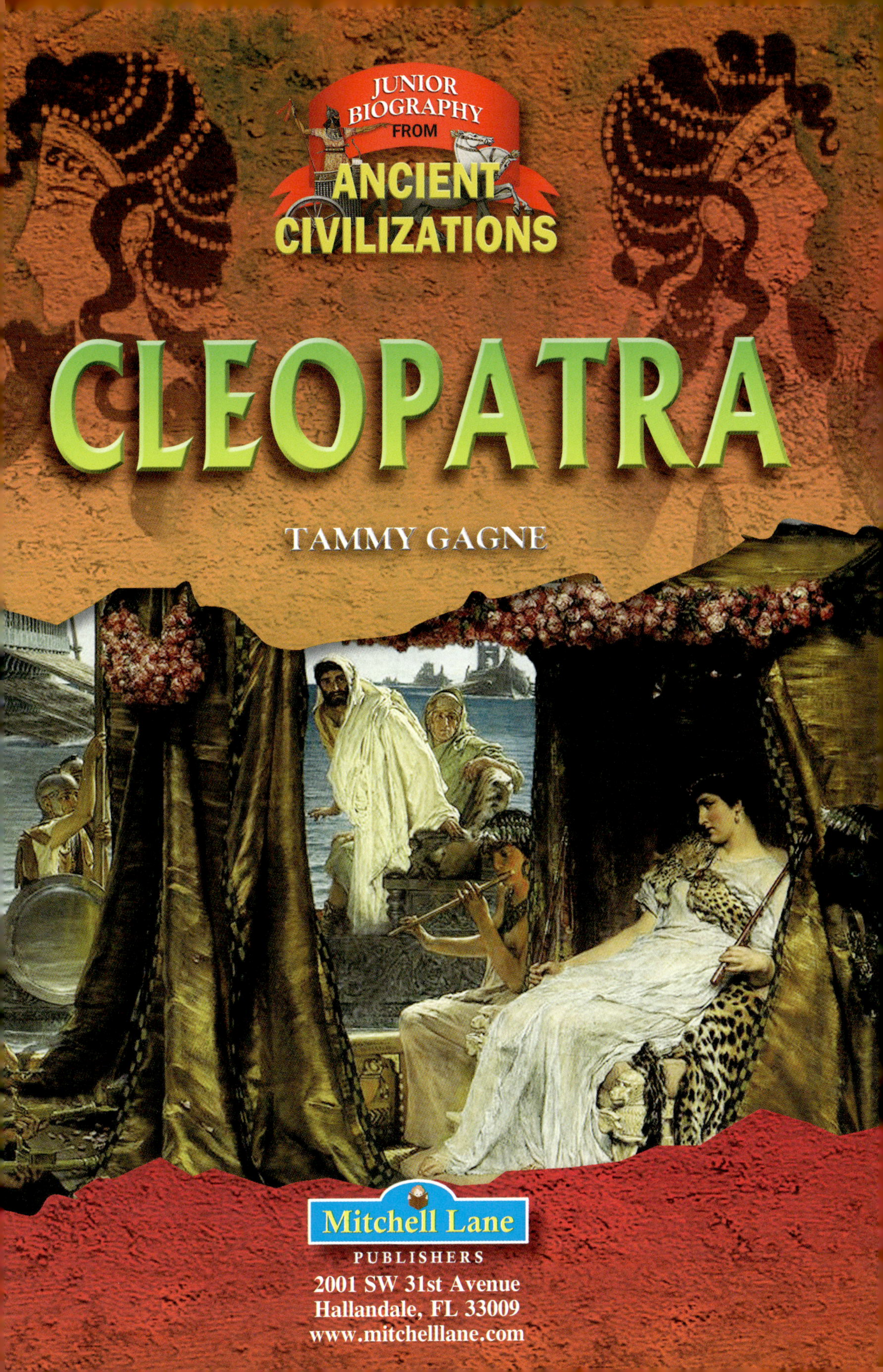
JUNIOR
BIOGRAPHY
FROM
ANCIENT
CIVILIZATIONS
CLEOPATRA
TAMMY GAGNE
Mitchell Lane
PUBLISHERS
2001 SW 31st Avenue
Hallandale, FL 33009
www.mitchelllane.com

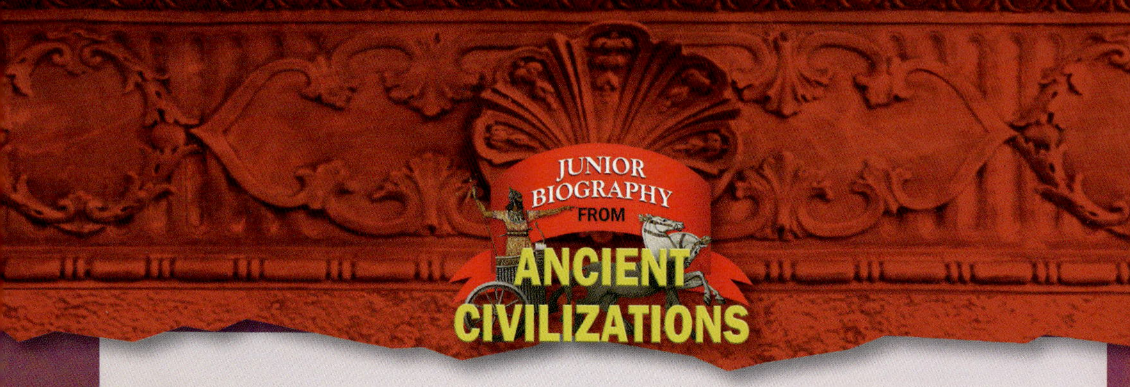

**Alexander the Great • Archimedes • Augustus Caesar
Buddha • Charlemagne • Cleopatra • Confucius
Genghis Khan • Hammurabi • Hippocrates • Homer
Julius Caesar • King Arthur • Leif Erikson • Marco Polo
Moses • Nero • Plato • Pythagoras • Socrates**

ABOUT THE AUTHOR: Tammy Gagne is the author of numerous books for adults and children, including *Buddha* and *King Arthur* for Mitchell Lane Publishers. She resides in northern New England with her husband and son. One of her favorite pastimes is visiting schools to speak to kids about the writing process.

PUBLISHER'S NOTE: The facts on which the story in this book is based have been thoroughly researched. Documentation of such research can be found on pages 45. While every possible effort has been made to ensure accuracy, the publisher will not assume liability for damages caused by inaccuracies in the data, and makes no warranty on the accuracy of the information contained herein.

To reflect current usage, we have chosen to use the secular era designations BCE ("before the common era") and CE ("of the common era") instead of the traditional designations BC ("before Christ") and AD (*anno Domini,* "in the year of the Lord").

Printing 1 2 3 4 5 6 7 8 9

**Library of Congress
Cataloging-in-Publication Data**

Names: Gagne, Tammy, author.
Title: Cleopatra / by Tammy Gagne.
Description: Hallandale, FL : Mitchell Lane Publishers, 2018. | Series: Junior biography from ancient civilizations | Includes bibliographical references and index.
Identifiers: LCCN 2017009111 | ISBN 9781680200225 (library bound)
Subjects: LCSH: Cleopatra, Queen of Egypt, -30 B.C.—Juvenile literature. | Queens—Egypt—Biography—Juvenile literature. | Egypt—History—332-30 B.C.—Juvenile literature.
Classification: LCC DT92.7 .G34 2018 | DDC 932/.021092 [B] —dc23
LC record available at https://lccn.loc.gov/2017009111

eBook ISBN: 978-1-618020-023-2

CONTENTS

Phonetic pronunciations of words in **bold** can be found on page 46.

Many women have portrayed the Egyptian Queen Cleopatra on stage and in films. This photo shows British actress Lillie Langtry when she starred in *Antony and Cleopatra.* The production was featured at London's Princess's Theatre in 1890.

CHAPTER 1
Finding the Truth

Cleopatra's* name is known throughout the world. Although she died more than two thousand years ago, Cleopatra's life is still the subject of numerous books and plays written by **Plutarch**, William Shakespeare, George Bernard Shaw, and others. Many glamorous stars on the silver screen have portrayed Cleopatra. Images of the Egyptian queen have been used in postage stamps, paintings, and statues. But what do we truly know about the woman we call Cleopatra? Was she as beautiful and bold as the legends about her maintain? Was she an evil enchantress or a shrewd mastermind?

The Greeks and the Romans wrote much of the information that has been unearthed about Cleopatra over the centuries. This isn't surprising. After all, Greek was the common language during Cleopatra's time. Nearly every Roman scholar knew how to speak and write Greek. Cleopatra was of Greek descent herself and spoke the language fluently. But Greek and Roman history may not be the most reliable source for accurate information about the Egyptian queen.

*For pronunciations of words in **bold**, see page 46.

CHAPTER 1

One of the benefits of winning a war is that the victor gets to write the history books. The only problem with this arrangement is that the winner's account of the enemy is one-sided. The Romans disliked Cleopatra immensely. They thought she possessed too much power, especially for a woman. They accused her of using her beauty to get what she wanted. And they dismissed her as self-indulgent and small-minded.

Certainly not everyone accepted the Romans' negative view of the Egyptian queen. A fair number of historians wanted to learn the true nature of Cleopatra. But it was nearly impossible for them to learn the ancient Egyptians' side of the story—at least at first. It wasn't until the nineteenth century that historians could even read Egyptian hieroglyphs.

The discovery of the Rosetta Stone in 1799 finally gave the world the means of understanding what those ancient symbols meant. But reliable translations took time. As the *Wall Street Journal* explained, "[The Rosetta Stone] featured texts in Greek, demotic [commonly spoken] Egyptian and hieroglyphics; the Greek indicated that the three passages were identical . . . But it wasn't until 1822 that **Jean-Francois Champollion** decoded the hieroglyphs."[1]

Scholars could also only study the artifacts that had been discovered. Egyptian history wasn't as neatly arranged as the books written by the Greeks. A little was found here; a bit more discovered there. Archaeologists and historians worked together to decipher the writings on various artifacts from Cleopatra's era. And as they did, they gradually assembled a new view into the lives of the ancient Egyptians and their beloved queen. This history had been recorded by the people who knew her best.

What most Greek accounts of her life overlooked was Cleopatra's impressive intelligence. "She was a very clever woman," wrote archaeologist Joyce Tyldesley. "She ruled for over 20 years and managed to delay the Romans taking over Egypt, which was something that was threatening throughout her reign. Plus, she took over a

The Rosetta Stone gave the modern world a much more detailed view of life in ancient Egypt. Until the discovery of this incredible artifact, most of what we knew about Cleopatra came from the Romans. As her enemy, they were not the best source of accurate information.

country from her father that was fairly poor and strengthened the economy so that when she died, Egypt was in a good position."[2]

While they held different opinions about Cleopatra, the Greeks and the Egyptians always appeared to agree on one thing: Everyone who encountered the queen found her especially captivating and fascinating. As Plutarch wrote, "[T]he charm of her presence was irresistible, and there was an attraction in her person and her talk, together with a peculiar force of character which pervaded her every word and action, that laid all who associated with her under her spell."[3]

A servant girl brings Cleopatra some fruit to eat.

The Missing Piece

The quality that most of the early texts about Cleopatra left out was how bright she was. Joyce Tyldesley, the author of *Cleopatra: Last Queen of Egyptians*, explained that the Romans did not simply overlook that important trait. Instead, Tyldesley thinks that they left it out on purpose. "There's a lie by default because few have ever credited her with being clever. She is mentioned in Arabic histories, where she is reported as an intelligent woman capable of many things."[4] The evidence supports this claim. The idea that Cleopatra relied on her looks to get what she wanted makes for more exciting stories. But the most thrilling tales can also distract the reader from the truth. As Tyldesley pointed out, "In a way, it's not as interesting when we get her back to who she really was—but of course, it makes her into a real person and not a stereotype, which is much better."[5]

A statue of Cleopatra on her deathbed

Some famous artists have depicted Cleopatra over the centuries. This drawing of the Egyptian queen was created by Michelangelo around 1532. Like many other Egyptian kings and queens, Cleopatra is strongly associated with snakes.

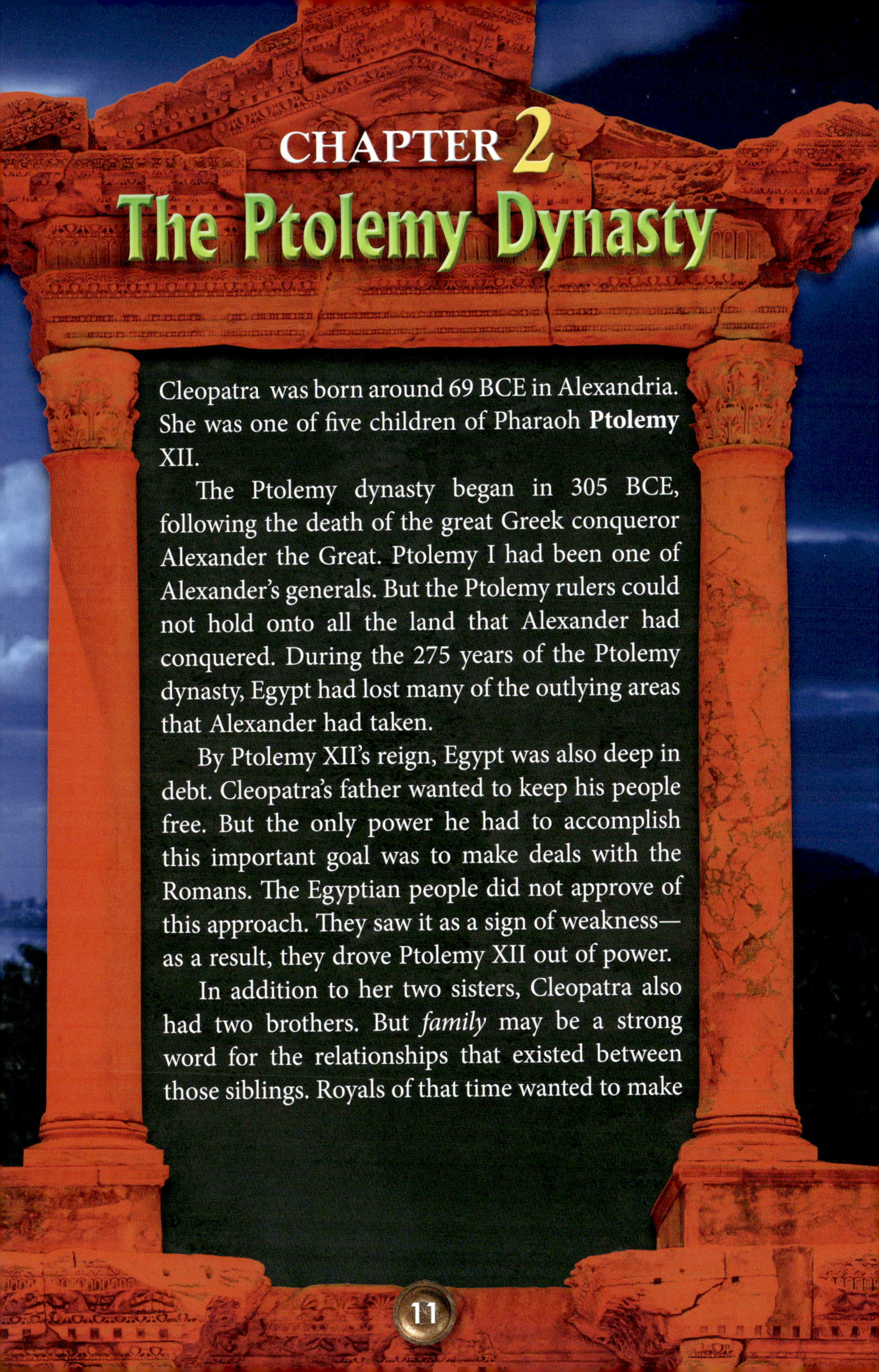

CHAPTER 2
The Ptolemy Dynasty

Cleopatra was born around 69 BCE in Alexandria. She was one of five children of Pharaoh **Ptolemy** XII.

The Ptolemy dynasty began in 305 BCE, following the death of the great Greek conqueror Alexander the Great. Ptolemy I had been one of Alexander's generals. But the Ptolemy rulers could not hold onto all the land that Alexander had conquered. During the 275 years of the Ptolemy dynasty, Egypt had lost many of the outlying areas that Alexander had taken.

By Ptolemy XII's reign, Egypt was also deep in debt. Cleopatra's father wanted to keep his people free. But the only power he had to accomplish this important goal was to make deals with the Romans. The Egyptian people did not approve of this approach. They saw it as a sign of weakness—as a result, they drove Ptolemy XII out of power.

In addition to her two sisters, Cleopatra also had two brothers. But *family* may be a strong word for the relationships that existed between those siblings. Royals of that time wanted to make sure their successors to the throne possessed all the best qualities. They believed the way to accomplish that goal was by marrying someone from their own bloodline—usually a brother or a sister. At the same time, competition for power was fierce. It wasn't unusual for one family member to kill another to gain power—and the throne.

Cleopatra's older sister, **Berenike** IV, was named queen in 58 BCE when Ptolemy XII went into exile. He returned three years later and murdered his own daughter to take back the throne from her.

Like her father, Cleopatra wasn't the first ruler with that name. She was the seventh and last Egyptian queen to bear that name. All the women of the Ptolemy dynasty were named Cleopatra, Berenike, or Arsinoe. But it is unlikely that Cleopatra was the daughter of Cleopatra VI. Most historians think Cleopatra's real mother was Cleopatra V, her father's second wife and sister.

Cleopatra was an intelligent young woman who stood out among the most powerful men and women of her day. Like her family members, she was educated in the Greek tradition. But as a ruler, she made many important efforts that her ancestors did not. The most famous queen of Egypt was said to speak nine languages. One of them was Egyptian. It is surprising that Cleopatra was the first of the Ptolemy family to learn the language of her people.

Dr. Joann Fletcher, author of *Cleopatra the Great: The Woman Behind the Legend* wrote, "The new monarch's ability to win hearts and minds had been greatly enhanced by her ability to speak to them directly in their own language, and as the first of her dynasty to learn Egyptian she had a deep understanding of their ancient culture."[1]

She also worshiped the Egyptian gods and goddesses. She showed a particular respect for Isis, the goddess of fertility. Over time the people even began to associate Cleopatra with that deity.

"She was the first monarch in several centuries to take such an active part in the rituals which gave Egypt its strength, and her decision had been inspired by Alexander's own attitude," Fletcher continued. "He too had celebrated traditional rites during his six-

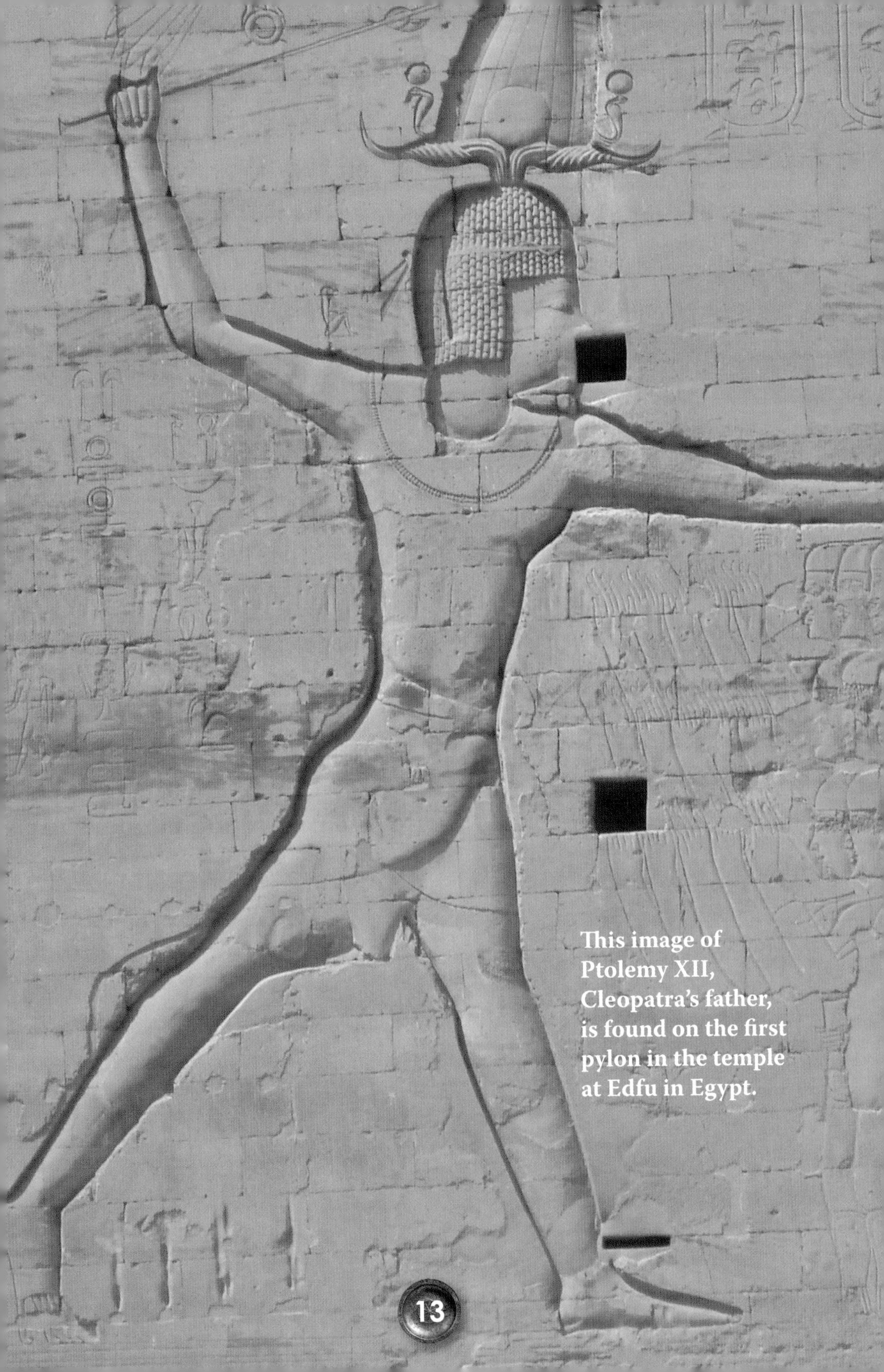

This image of Ptolemy XII, Cleopatra's father, is found on the first pylon in the temple at Edfu in Egypt.

month stay in Egypt, [honoring] the ancient deities and paying homage to the sacred creatures that contained the souls of the very gods themselves."[2]

Cleopatra began by paying tribute to Buchis, the bull god. Just days into her reign, the queen began a journey south to Hermonthis, near Thebes. While there she would not only attend but also lead an event that honored Buchis. Duane W. Roller, author of a biography of the Egyptian queen, noted that although the event had been held for thousands of years, Cleopatra was also "the first Ptolemy to attend this ceremony in person. The journey of more than four hundred miles up the Nile also served to make her visible to her new subjects."[3]

This fragment of a statue of Cleopatra is in the Royal Ontario Museum in Ontario, Canada.

Self-Confident or Self-Absorbed?

Some modern psychiatrists (doctors who study the mind) who have studied Cleopatra have suggested that she might have been mentally ill. They think she suffered from a disorder called a narcissistic personality. This condition was named after a vain character from Greek mythology who was so taken with his own looks that he fell in love with his reflection. If true, the psychiatrists' claim means that the Egyptian queen could only understand the world and the people in it as they related to her own circumstances.

But Dr. Joann Fletcher didn't accept that conclusion. Instead, she saw Cleopatra's high self-esteem as a product of her royal upbringing. Yes, Cleopatra was confident. But "she had been raised as a goddess from birth," Fletcher wrote, "and such traits are hardly surprising in a descendant of Alexander and three centuries of monarchs who believed themselves divine and [who] were worshipped by their people . . . the supreme self-confidence that such belief gave Cleopatra was clearly most attractive."[4]

Cleopatra by John William Waterhouse

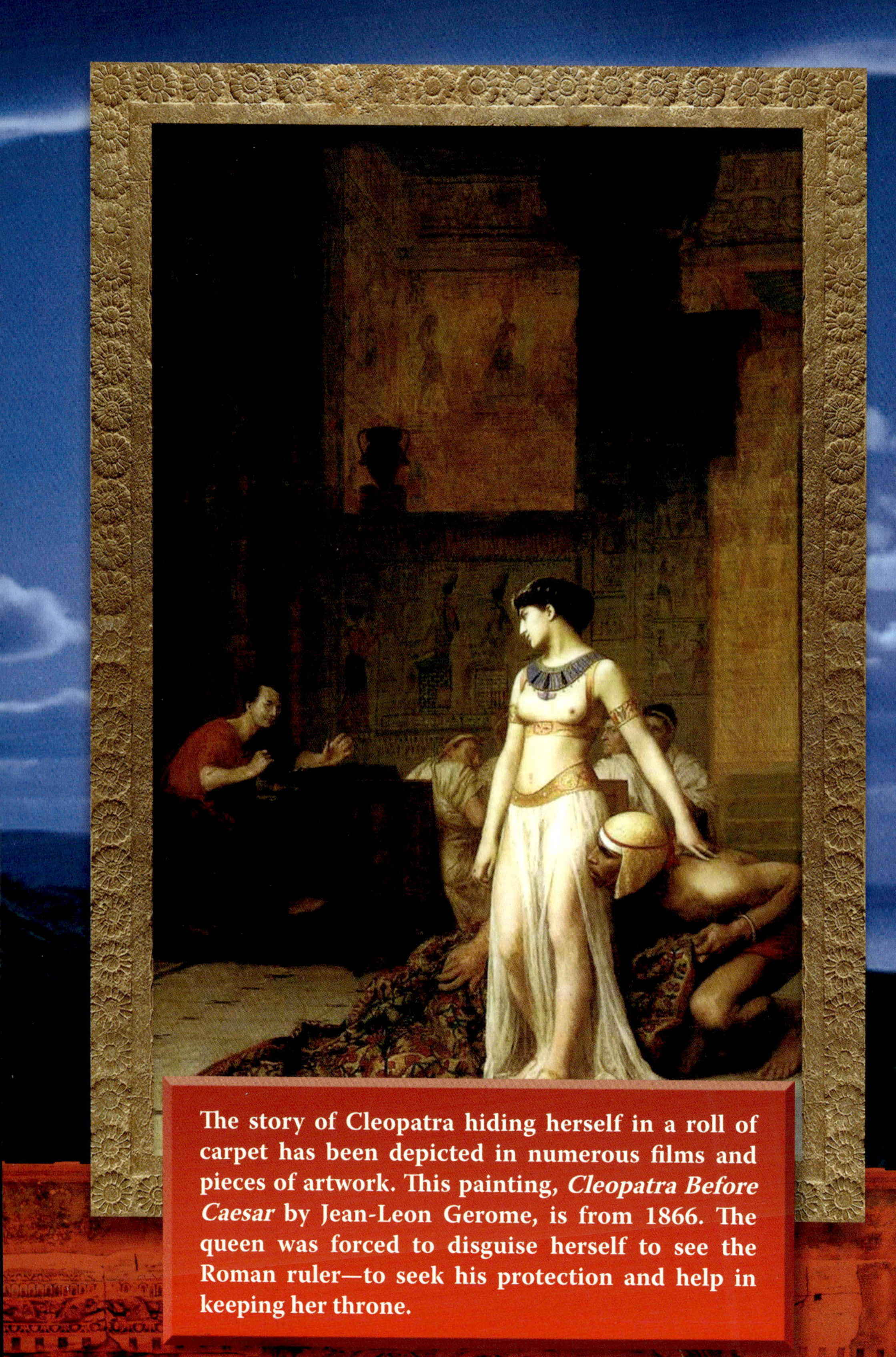

The story of Cleopatra hiding herself in a roll of carpet has been depicted in numerous films and pieces of artwork. This painting, *Cleopatra Before Caesar* by Jean-Leon Gerome, is from 1866. The queen was forced to disguise herself to see the Roman ruler—to seek his protection and help in keeping her throne.

CHAPTER 3
Cleopatra and Caesar

Cleopatra intimidated the Romans. The Egyptian queen was unlike anyone they had ever seen. Roman women did not serve in commanding positions. Men controlled the Senate, which was the empire's government, and Roman men were also in charge of their families. The Romans were wary of a woman who had so much power.

The documentary *Cleopatra: The First Woman of Power* examined the life of the Egyptian queen and how the Romans viewed her. "They were worried because she was something larger than life —something mythic, something terrifying . . ."[1] The film noted that other powerful women had been part of the Ptolemy dynasty, "but none dared claim the throne for herself."[2]

When 18-year-old Cleopatra took over the throne when her father died in 51 BCE, she was forced to marry her 10-year-old brother Ptolemy XIII. At first it seemed that they would rule Egypt together. But her younger sibling soon turned against her. Cleopatra likely had no intention of sharing her power anyway. The pair began a very public battle for sole control of the throne.

Caesar Giving Cleopatra the Throne of Egypt **by Pietro da Cortona shows the Roman ruler giving Cleopatra his official blessing to continue in her role as the queen of the Egyptian people. The act was seen as a joining of the Roman and Egyptian empires.**

Accounts of Cleopatra's appearance vary significantly. Some history books insist that she was incredibly beautiful. The Romans insisted that she used her beauty and charm to control some of the most powerful men of the ancient world. Roman writers claimed that she was indeed especially attractive. But other accounts of the queen's looks are far less kind. Many described her as having a large nose. That was a common trait among the Ptolemy monarchs.

According to the documentary, "Nearly every image of Cleopatra from her own time has been lost. Only three busts remain." One of them shows an attractive but unremarkable young woman. "The hair is swept back in a bun. The large nose and the wide royal hairband identify the queen."[3] Fletcher suggested that the real Cleopatra might not have looked at all like the image we have become used to seeing. "Cleopatra may well have been a redhead, judging from the portrait of a flame-haired woman wearing the royal diadem, surrounded by Egyptian motifs which has been identified as Cleopatra."[4]

While people still debate whether Cleopatra used beauty, charm, or intelligence to influence other powerful people, no one denies that she succeeded. When Julius Caesar came to Egypt in 48 BCE, he was instantly impressed with the young Egyptian queen. In order to secure a private meeting with him, Cleopatra is said to have concealed herself in a rolled carpet which she had delivered to Caesar's quarters. Although Caesar was married and more than 30 years older than the queen, the pair began a love affair.

Some historians say that Caesar probably saw a bit of himself in the young queen. She was one of the few people as ambitious as he was. And like Cleopatra, Caesar also had a reputation for being able to persuade the opposite sex with his charm. The Romans sang a song about him, which advised men to lock their wives away when Caesar arrived.

Caesar had come to Egypt to protect Rome's financial interests. When Cleopatra's father died, he was deeply in debt to the Romans. Caesar knew that a civil war would do nothing to help him recover that debt. At first it seemed that he wanted the fighting between the queen and her brother to end. He even ordered them to rule together peacefully. But when it became apparent that that wasn't going to happen, Caesar quickly took Cleopatra's side in the fight. Ptolemy XIII was soon found dead, drowned in the Nile River.

Cleopatra's only surviving brother (Ptolemy XIV) was only 12 at that time. But as tradition demanded, she married her younger sibling. Officially, the marriage made him her new co-ruler. But the child's ruling position was in name only. Cleopatra continued to rule Egypt alone. That brother also eventually ended up dead, "probably murdered on her orders."[5]

The new plan appeared to be a joining of the Roman and Egyptian empires. It looked like Cleopatra would regain the larger kingdom Egypt had once had under Alexander. Some say that Caesar and Cleopatra even planned to expand their newly joined empires into Asia.

Less than a year after meeting Caesar, Cleopatra gave birth to his first child. The Egyptians called him **Caesarion**, after the man believed to be his father. But Caesar never acknowledged the child officially. Even when he invited Cleopatra and Caesarion to visit him in Rome, he never claimed the boy as his son.

Caesar hoped that his fellow Romans would accept and honor the Egyptian queen. He even ordered a golden statue of her to be built. Caesar had it placed in the Roman temple of Venus, the Roman version of Isis. Cleopatra fascinated the Roman people. But they remained suspicious of her.

Fletcher said that Cleopatra arrived in Rome dressed stunningly and decorated with expensive jewels. "Cleopatra's appearance that night was noteworthy and contrasted to the plain-looking matrons of Caesar's Rome,"[6] according to Fletcher. Roman law allowed women to wear no more than half an ounce of gold jewelry. Instead of resisting this limitation, they embraced it. They considered jewels to be indulgent. The Romans themselves described Cleopatra as "painted up beyond all measure" and "weighed down by her adornments."[7] They saw her as a spoiled and shallow young woman who was only concerned with herself.

More than Face Value

Ancient coins bearing Cleopatra's image have long been a source of debate about her true appearance. Some of those ancient currencies depicted her as having almost manlike features. Others made the young queen look old and unattractive. Since coins were created upon monarchs' orders, one might find it hard to believe that Cleopatra would approve such unflattering images of herself. But it is important to consider that coins of this era were especially simple. Capturing an accurate portrait on such a small token would have been a difficult feat. Cleopatra also might have wanted to send a message with those altered likenesses. Perhaps she wanted to depict herself as more masculine or mature to the people who thought that a young woman wasn't capable of ruling a country. She might have thought that she would be taken more seriously if her critics saw her as she appeared on the coins.

An Egyptian coin of Cleopatra minted around 40 BCE

A Greek coin of Cleopatra

This papyrus painting of Cleopatra with the ancient Egyptian god Horus is just one example of how the queen was associated with the Egyptian goddess Isis. Horus was the goddess's son, so this piece of art depicted the queen as a motherly figure.

CHAPTER 4
The Mother of a Nation

The Egyptians held an entirely different view of Cleopatra from the Romans. They saw her as caring about their problems. She gave them plenty of reasons to have a high opinion of her.

The ancient Egyptians called the Nile River the *Ar* or *Aur*, which means "black." The reason was the dark-colored silt that the river left behind when it flooded each year. While most people in the world think of flooding as a bad thing, in that area of the world the rising water actually had tremendous value. Egypt has an especially dry climate. But the silt left by the flooding made the soil rich enough to grow crops.

During Cleopatra's reign, though, the flooding had lessened significantly. Author Stacy Schiff explained, "The country's well-being depended entirely on the height of the flood . . ."[1] When a drought occurred, food became scarce. People who lived in Alexandria faced a higher risk of starving, as they depended on food grown in rural areas. But when the farmers didn't have enough food, they couldn't send food north to the city dwellers.

Cleopatra knew that she would be judged harshly if she could not feed her people. "Hungry Alexandrians were more dangerous than hungry villagers; it was in everyone's best interest to appease them,"[2] Schiff said. Cleopatra declared a state of emergency, ordering farmers to send a certain amount of wheat and dry vegetables north. Schiff adds that "Offenders received a death sentence."[3] She also offered rewards to people who agreed to stay in or move to rural areas to help increase the food supply.

Cleopatra's people continued to idolize her. Many even saw her as a human reincarnation of Isis. She wasn't the first Ptolemy queen who had a connection to the goddess. Many women before had also forged a strong link to the female deity. But that link was strong with Cleopatra. She dressed as Isis on important occasions. She was good at creating publicity for herself.

When Caesarion was born, Cleopatra made great efforts to compare their mother-and-son relationship with that of Isis and the goddess' infant son Horus. She issued coins with Caesarion depicted as Horus. She wanted her people to see her as a motherly figure. But that wasn't the only point—Isis was a symbol of female power. "In some accounts," wrote Schiff, "Isis grants women the same strength as men."[4]

Cleopatra was indeed a strong woman, but she knew that she needed a strong ally in Rome. She had been raised during an especially difficult time for Egypt, and she quickly learned that money could solve many problems. Her father's

Isis with Horus the Child at Walter's Art Museum in Baltimore, Maryland

Egyptian images of Cleopatra and her son Caesarion at the Temple of Dendera

reign had proved to her that a lack of money made many situations worse. She was determined not to repeat his mistakes. While she may have truly cared about Julius Caesar, she also knew that the Roman Empire could help improve the situation of the Egyptian people.

What she didn't realize was that Caesar's own people were growing fearful of him. Some worried that he wanted to do away with the Roman Senate and rule as a king. In 44 BCE, a group of Roman senators murdered him to prevent that from happening. The powerful ruler whom Cleopatra had counted on to protect her from the Romans was gone.

Following Caesar's death, Cleopatra named her young son her co-ruler. She hoped that together they could hold onto Egypt—and perhaps even extend their empire farther across the Mediterranean Sea. She continued to compare herself to the goddess Isis. Like Cleopatra, Isis had a mate who was murdered. The queen ordered the creation of massive monuments that looked like giant stone billboards. On one of them, Cleopatra and Caesarion stood opposite Isis, Horus, and the goddess' mate, **Osiris**. The message was clear: The Egyptian queen was just like Isis—and her son was the heir to the Roman throne.

Osiris with an Atef-crown made of bronze in the Museum of Natural History in Vienna, Austria

The Son of Caesar

No one knows for certain whether Julius Caesar ever acknowledged Caesarion as his son. But many historians think that the Roman ruler was planning to do just that before he was murdered. Caesar's Roman wife **Calpurnia** had not given him any children. And having an heir—a son in particular—was surely an important goal for such a powerful man.

Dr. Joann Fletcher wrote, "Cleopatra's son must have been a particularly proud achievement in Caesar's Roman world, where male children were considered far superior to girls. Announcing the news of his fatherhood to his close associates **Gaius Matinus** and **Gaius Oppius**, Caesar also began to contemplate plans for a new law which would make it legal for him to have more than one marriage for the purpose of producing an heir—clear evidence of the serious nature of his relationship with Cleopatra and his intentions for their son."[5]

Caesarion, from the Cleopatra exhibit, "Unravel the Mystery," at the Franklin Institute in Philadelphia

Following the death of Julius Caesar, Marcus Antony would change Cleopatra's life in many ways. Their historic meeting is illustrated in this painting by Giovanni Battista Tiepolo.

CHAPTER 5
Cleopatra's Downfall

When Julius Caesar's will was read, neither Cleopatra nor Caesarion was mentioned. Since Caesar and his wife Calpurnia had no children, he named his nephew, **Octavian**, as his heir. Cleopatra wasn't the only one who was surprised by that turn of events. **Marcus Antony**, who had served in the Roman Senate, had been a trusted friend of Caesar's. But the ruler completely overlooked him in naming his successor.

Antony was determined not to give up his position in the Senate. He also insisted on controlling the money left by Caesar. The people of Rome were divided when it came to Octavian and Antony. And for a while the two Romans had a rather public battle for the public's approval. Soon, though, both men realized that the empire needed a united government if it was going to continue to thrive. The men joined forces with **Marcus Lepidus**, forming a triumvirate.

Still, Antony had a poor reputation. He was known for being self-indulgent. Some of the Romans suspected that he had stolen from Octavian's inheritance to pay his own debts. He

Cleopatra and Octavian **by Louis Gauffier shows the Egyptian queen and the newly named Roman leader, Octavian. As part of his will, Caesar chose his nephew as his successor.**

was also known for having little control when it came to both alcohol and women. He was married to his third wife when he sent a letter to Cleopatra in 41 BCE. In it he asked to meet with the Egyptian queen.

The 28-year-old Cleopatra was wary at first. She put Antony off for many weeks before finally agreeing to meet him in Tarsus, in what is now Turkey. Once the two finally met, however, Cleopatra made a huge impression on the Roman. Traveling through the Mediterranean on the royal barge, she dressed like **Aphrodite**, the Greek goddess of love. And like Caesar, Antony was completely in awe of Cleopatra at first sight.

Antony seemed like a second chance at both love and greater power for the queen. She soon gave birth to twins **Alexander Helios** and **Cleopatra Selene**. The couple later welcomed a third child named **Ptolemy Philadelphus**. Once again there were problems. Although Antony's wife soon died, he gave in to pressure to marry Octavian's sister instead of staying with Cleopatra and their children. Again, it looked like Cleopatra had lost her hold on Rome. But she wasn't ready to give up.

Hearing that Antony was in Syria during the fall of 37 BCE, Cleopatra traveled to meet him there. They remained together through the winter. During that time, she convinced him that his power and her resources could help the two of them take Rome for themselves. She offered to supply Antony with money, ships, and men. Upon his return home, Antony announced that Caesarion was the true heir to Julius Caesar, and to the Roman Empire itself.

Octavian told the Roman people that Antony had been manipulated by the Egyptian queen. He immediately stripped Antony of all his political power and declared war on Cleopatra. The fate of both empires depended on which side emerged the victor.

The conflict came to a head in the summer of 31 BCE. Octavian's forces—led by the brilliant general **Agrippa**—had blockaded Cleopatra and Antony at Actium. It was a Roman colony on the west coast of Greece. Supplies began running low and many men fell ill. So their combined fleets tried to break out on the morning of September 2. Their ships were larger than Octavian's but not as maneuverable. During the confusion of the battle, Cleopatra took advantage of a breeze that sprang up. Her 60 ships managed to escape. Antony followed her with a handful of his ships. The others had to surrender. Antony had proven himself loyal to Cleopatra. But his

When Cleopatra finally agreed to meet with Marcus Antony, she traveled to Tarsus—now Turkey. Claude Lorrain painted *The Disembarkation of Cleopatra at Tarsus* in honor of the journey.

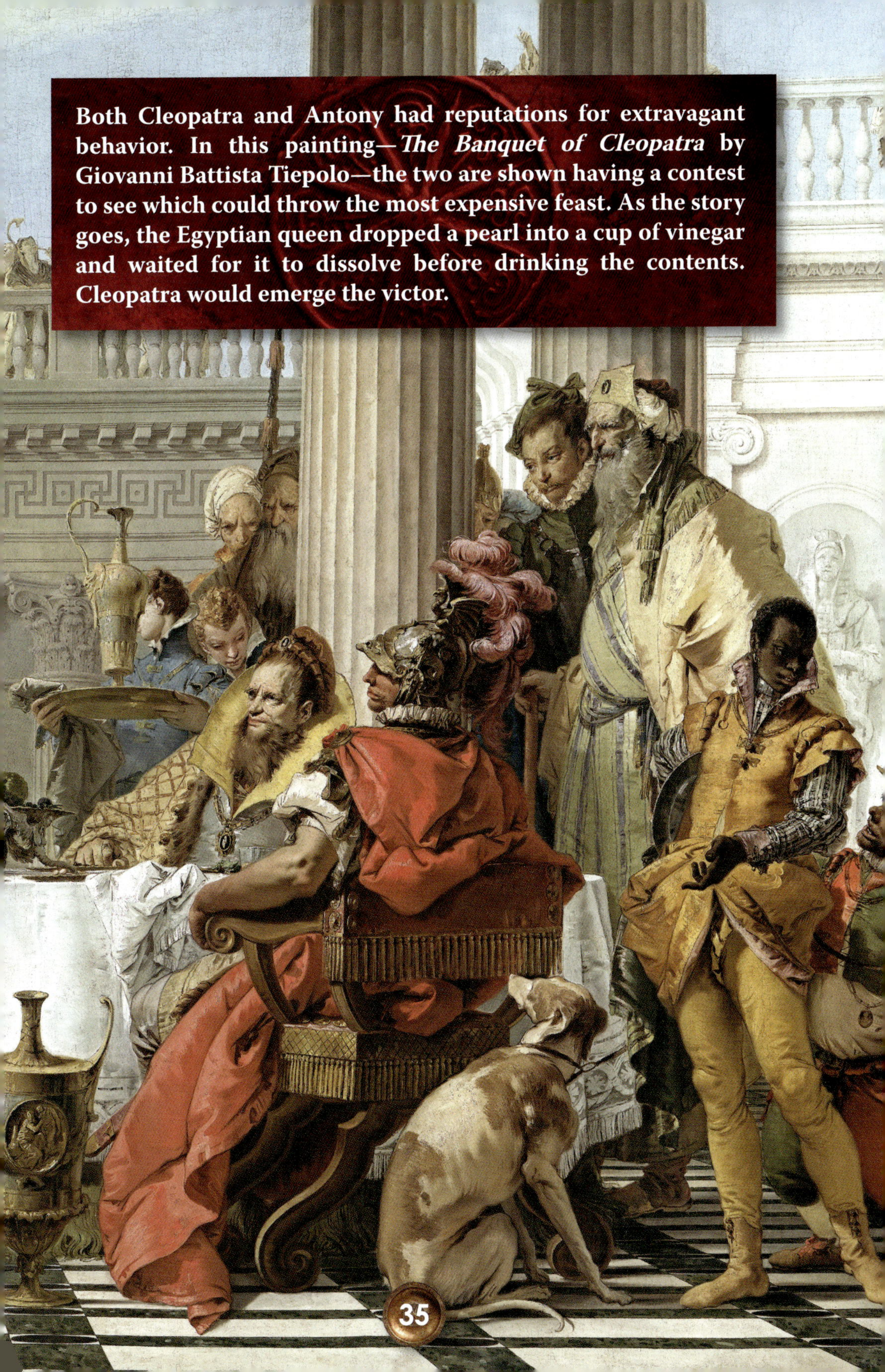

Both Cleopatra and Antony had reputations for extravagant behavior. In this painting—*The Banquet of Cleopatra* by Giovanni Battista Tiepolo—the two are shown having a contest to see which could throw the most expensive feast. As the story goes, the Egyptian queen dropped a pearl into a cup of vinegar and waited for it to dissolve before drinking the contents. Cleopatra would emerge the victor.

The Battle of Actium would mark the beginning of the end for Cleopatra and Marcus Antony. They chose to retreat when it became clear that they could not beat Octavian. The Roman Empire would never be theirs as the pair had hoped.

loyalty—even combined with their once-massive fleet—could not win the Roman Empire for them.

The documentary *Cleopatra: The First Woman of Power* stated, "She had to make the best she could of him. And she made the best she could of him. And it wasn't enough."[1]

Cleopatra and Antony returned to Alexandria together. But their days were numbered. In the spring of 30 BCE, Octavian led his army to Egypt to remove Cleopatra from power. The documentary continued, "She offers to abdicate if her children can rule in her place. Marcus Antony offers his life to save Cleopatra. Octavian ignores their pleas."[2]

When the fighting began, it looked like Cleopatra and Antony had a chance at victory. But Octavian once again got the upper hand. When Antony heard a rumor that Cleopatra was dead, he stabbed himself in grief. Shortly thereafter his men located the queen—still very much alive—and brought him to her. He died in her arms. Cleopatra had now lost both the men she had loved.

Knowing that the end of her rule was near, the queen refused to allow her enemy to take her alive. Cleopatra committed suicide after asking to be buried alongside Antony. Some people say that she used a poisonous snake to bring about her death. But that has never been proven. Joyce Tyldesley stated, "The nearest we have to an eye-witness, which was actually written hundreds of years later, says she had puncture marks on her arm—that could be anything or nothing at all. But it's a nice story, because everyone seems to hate snakes."[3]

Cleopatra's story ended in tragedy but her reign had been an important one. She was recorded in history as "A queen who reconstructed her country, a working queen, and a queen who kept Rome at bay for twenty years."[4]

Cleopatra statue at the Rosicrucian Egyptian Museum in San Jose, California

This painting by Alexandre Bida shows Antony dying in Cleopatra's arms.

The Fate of Those who Remained

Following Cleopatra's death, Octavian ordered his men to hunt down Caesarion and kill him. If the teenager was indeed the son of the late Julius Caesar, he posed an enormous threat to Octavian's political power. Even if the Romans didn't embrace Caesarion as Caesar's true heir, the boy could one day challenge Octavian for control of Rome and he might fare better than his mother and Antony had. Caesarion was killed.

Octavian spared the lives of Cleopatra's three other children. According to *The Berkshire Eagle*, "[They] were sent to Rome and put under the care of Octavian's sister, Octavia, Antony's wife. Cleopatra Selene married King Juba II of Mauretania. No one knows what happened to Alexander Helios or Ptolemy Philadelphus."[5]

Octavian turned Egypt into a province of the Empire. He went on to become Rome's first emperor, and took the name **Augustus Caesar**. He ruled until his own death in 14 CE.

A bronze statue of Augustus Caesar at Augsburg City Hall in Augsburg, Germany

69 BCE	Cleopatra VII is born.
51	Cleopatra becomes queen, marrying her younger brother, Ptolemy XIII.
48	Julius Caesar comes to Egypt and helps Cleopatra become the sole ruler.
44	Julius Caesar is murdered.
42	Marcus Antonius (Marc Antony) meets Cleopatra.
32	Octavian removes Antony from power.
31	Octavian defeats Cleopatra and Antony in the Battle of Actium.
30	Cleopatra and Antony commit suicide. Octavian takes Egypt for Rome.

The Death of Cleopatra by Juan Luna

TIMELINE

332 BCE	Alexander the Great conquers Egypt.
305	Ptolemy I becomes pharaoh and the Ptolemy Dynasty begins.
196	The Rosetta Stone is carved.
30	Egypt becomes part of the Roman Empire.
642 CE	Egypt is conquered by the Arabs.

This mummy in the British Museum in London, England, may be Cleopatra's remains.

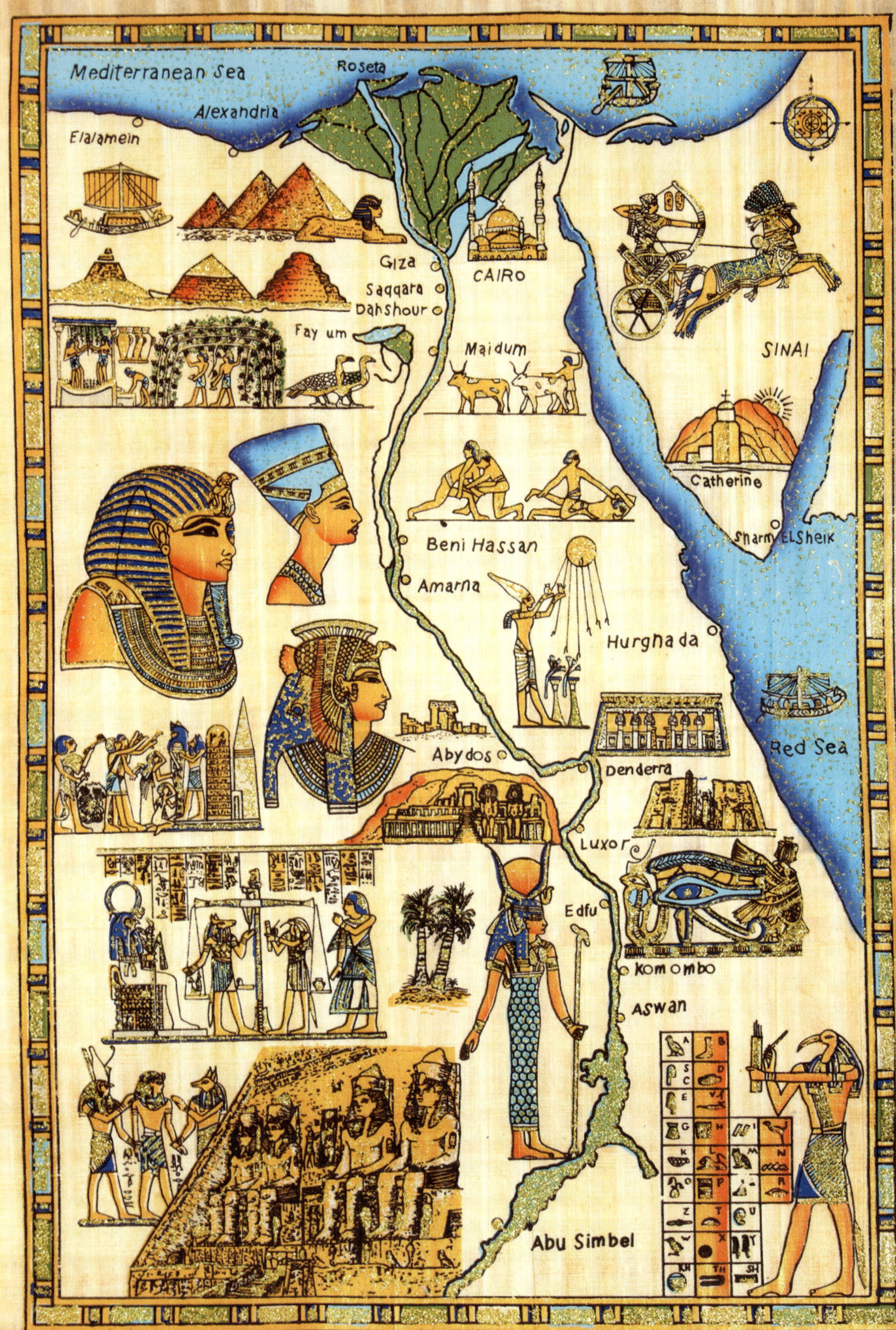

This papyrus map of ancient Egypt depicts its most important sites.

Chapter 1 Finding the Truth

1. Howard Schneider, "Book Review: 'Egyptomania.' " *Wall Street Journal*, November 29, 2013. http://www.wsj.com/news/articles/SB10001424052702303914304579191873770811000.
2. The Real Cleopatra." BBC, September 24, 2014. http://www.bbc.co.uk/manchester/content/articles/2008/01/24/240108_cleopatra_feature.shtml
3. "Myths of Cleopatra." *Al-Ahram Weekly*, no. 1206, July 17, 2014. http://weekly.ahram.org.eg/News/6808/23/Myths-of-Cleopatra.aspx
4. "The Real Cleopatra," BBC, September 24, 2014. http://www.bbc.co.uk/manchester/content/articles/2008/01/24/240108_cleopatra_feature.shtml
5. Ibid.

Chapter 2 The Ptolemy Dynasty

1. Joann Fletcher, *Cleopatra the Great: The Woman Behind the Legend* (New York: Harper Collins, 2008), p. 13.
2. Ibid.
3. Duane Roller. *Cleopatra: A Biography* (Oxford, England: Oxford University Press, 2010), p. 53.
4. Fletcher, *Cleopatra the Great*, p. 106.

Chapter 3 Cleopatra and Caesar

1. "Cleopatra: The First Woman of Power," Discovery Channel (1999). Video.
2. Ibid.
3. Ibid.
4. Joann Fletcher, *Cleopatra the Great: The Woman Behind the Legend* (New York: Harper Collins, 2008), p. 87.
5. "Cleopatra: The First Woman of Power."
6. Fletcher, *Cleopatra the Great*, p. 115.
7. Ibid., p. 116.

Chapter 4. The Mother of a Nation

1. Stacy Schiff, *Cleopatra: A Life* (New York: Little, Brown and Company, 2010), p. 55.
2. Ibid.
3. Ibid.
4. Schiff, *Cleopatra,* p. 87.
5. Joann Fletcher. *Cleopatra the Great: The Woman Behind the Legend* (New York: Harper Collins, 2008), p. 162.

Chapter 5. Cleopatra's Downfall

1. "Cleopatra: The First Woman of Power," Discovery Channel (1999), Video.
2. Ibid.
3. "The Real Cleopatra," BBC, September 24, 2014. http://www.bbc.co.uk/manchester/content/articles/2008/01/24/240108_cleopatra_feature.shtml
4. "Cleopatra: The First Woman of Power."
5. Gary Clothier, "Mr. Know it All: Cleopatra's legacy shrouded in mystery." Uexpress, November 20, 2013. http://www.uexpress.com/ask-mr-know-it-all/2013/11/20/cleopatras-legacy-shrouded-in-mystery

Books

Blackaby, Susan. *Cleopatra: Egypt's Last and Greatest Queen*. New York: Sterling Publishing, 2009.

Norwich, Grace. *I Am Cleopatra*. New York: Scholastic, 2014.

Schecter, Vicky Alvear. *Cleopatra Rules!* Honesdale, Pennsylvania: Boyds Mill Press, 2011.

Works Consulted

Fletcher, Joann. *Cleopatra the Great: The Woman Behind the Legend*. New York: Harper Collins Publishers, 2008.

Lorenzi, Rosella. "Cleopatra and Antony's Children Rediscovered." Discovery News. April 20, 2012. http://news.discovery.com/history/archaeology/cleopatras-twin-babies-120420.htm.

Grant, Michael. *Cleopatra: A Biography by Michael Grant*. New York: Simon and Schuster, 1972.

Roller, Duane W. *Cleopatra: A Biography*. Oxford, England: Oxford University Press, 2010.

Schiff, Stacy. *Cleopatra: A Life*. New York: Little, Brown and Company, 2010.

On the Internet

Cleopatra
http://www.history.com/topics/ancient-history/cleopatra

Cleopatra: The Woman Behind the Name
http://www.touregypt.net/cleopatra.htm

Cleopatra VII Biography
http://www.biography.com/people/cleopatra-vii-9250984

PHONETIC PRONUNCIATIONS

Agrippa (uh-GRIP-puh)
Alexander Helios (al-ix-ZAN-der HEE-lee-ohs)
Aphrodite (af-roh-DI-tee)
Augustus Caesar (uh-GUHS-tuhs SEE-zer)
Berenike (bahy-reh-NI-kee)
Caesarion (she-SAHYR-ee-uhn)
Calpurnia (kal-PUR-nee-uh)
Cleopatra (klee-oh-PAH-truh)
Cleopatra Selene (klee-oh-PAH-truh seh-LEEN)
Gaius Matinus (GUY-uhs MAH-tin-uhs)
Gaius Oppius (GUY-uhs AW-pee-uhs)
Jean-Francois Champollion (jahn-fran-SWAH sham-POH-lee-ohn)
Julius Caesar (JOO-lee-uhs SEE-zer)
Marcus Antony (MAHR-kus AN-toh-nee)
Marcus Lepidus (MAHR-kus LEP-ih-duhs)
Marcus (MAHR-kus)
Octavian (awk-TAHY-vee-uhn)
Osiris (oh-SI-ruhs)
Plutarch (PLOO-tark)
Ptolemy (TAHL-uh-mee)
Ptolemy Philadelphus (TAHL-uh-mee fil-uh-DEL-fus)

PHOTO CREDITS: Cover, p. 1—Lawrence Alma-Tadema/public domain; p. 4—Photos.com/Thinkstock; p. 7—Hans Hillewaert/cc-by sa 4.0; p. 8—CoreyFord/Thinkstock; p. 9—ggenova/Thinkstock; p. 10—Michelangelo/Public domain; p. 13—cc-by sa; p. 14—Daderot/public domain; p. 15—John William Waterhouse/public domain; p. 16—Jean-Léon Gérôme/public domain; p. 18—Pietro da Cortona/public domain; p. 21—PHGCOM/public domain; pp. 22, 42—Edwardgerges/Dreamstime; p. 24—Henry Walters/Walter Art Museum/cc-by-sa 3.0; p. 25—William McKelvie/Thinkstock; p. 26—Marco Almbauer/cc-by sa 3.0; p. 27—Sdwelch1031/public domain; pp. 28, 34–35—Giovanni Battista Tiepolo/public domain; p. 30—Louis Gauffier/public domain; pp. 32–33—Claude Lorrain/public domain; p. 36—Laureys a Castro/public domain; p. 37—cc-by sa; p. 38—Alexandre Bida/Folger Shakespeare Library/cc-by sa 4.0; p. 39—FooTToo/Thinkstock; p. 40—Juan Luna/public domain; p. 41—Robot Brainz/cc-by 2.0.

abdicate (AB-di-kaat)—to formally give up sovereign power, office, or responsibility

archeologist (AR-ke-OL-e-jist)—a person who studies past human life as shown by fossil relics and the monuments and tools left by ancient peoples

bust—a piece of sculpture representing the upper part of the human figure including the head and neck

deity (DEE-i-tee)—a god or goddess

drought (DROUT)—a long period of dry weather

dynasty (DII-ne-stee)—a succession of rulers from the same family

exile (EG-ziel)—being forced to leave one's country or home

hieroglyphs (HIGH-uhr-oh-glifs)—pictures used as characters in ancient Egyptian writing

manipulate (me-NIP-ye-laat)—to manage or control with intent to deceive

matron (MAY-tren)—a usually mature and dignified married woman

narcissism (NAHR-se-SIZ-em)—a personality disorder involving excessive self-love

publicity (pu-BLIS-i-tee)—taking action that causes public notice, for example, putting up monuments or getting in the news

silt (SILT)—fine sand carried by water

stereotype (STARE-ee-oh-type)—an idea that many people have about a thing or a group and that may often be untrue or only partly true

triumvirate (try-UHM-vihr-it)—government by three persons who share authority and responsibility